Memories...
simply the best

memories...simply the best:

Rain or rainbows...
I'll be near...♥

Place photo here

Wherever you go,
in sunshine or shadow,
may your memories be of
days filled with happiness,
love, laughter, and friends.

Place photo here

memories... memories...simply the best

memories...simply the best:

Hugs & warm wishes...sweet little kisses...
XOXO

Place photo here

Memories grow a day at a time.
And each day, a new memory
blossoms to be cherished for
many years to come.

Place photo here

memories…simply the best:

_____

_____

_____

_____

_____

_____

_____

_____

You can count on friends…
when you need a help up….

Place photo here

As your friendships grow,
so will your memories!

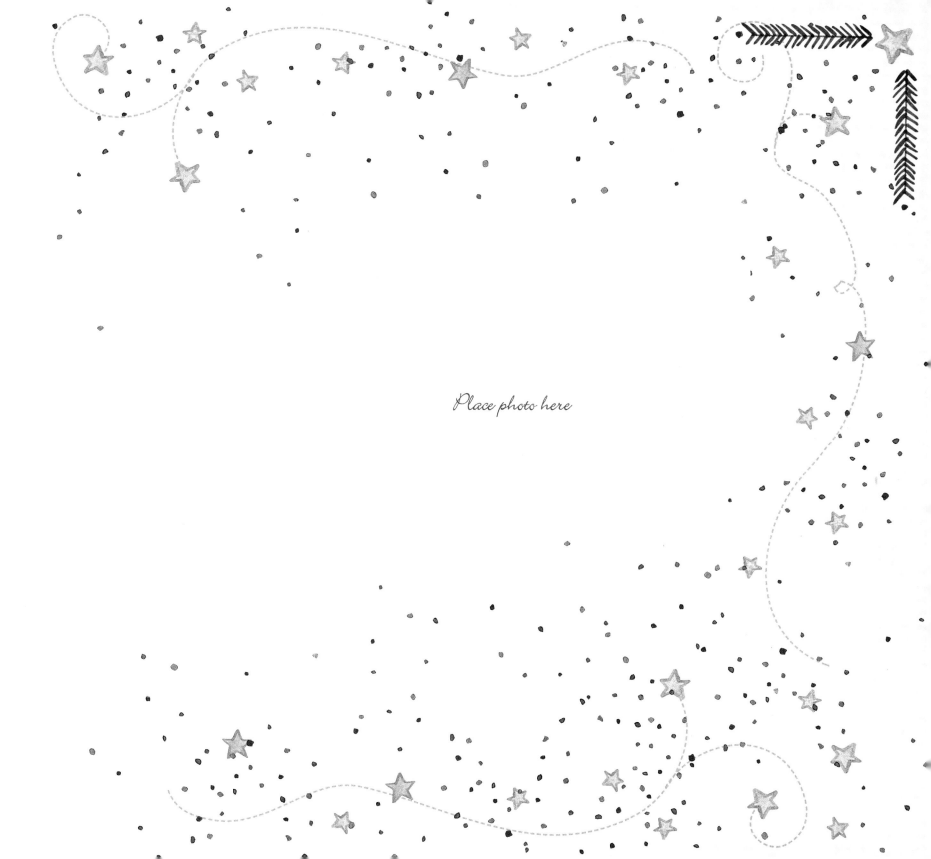

Place photo here

memories...simply the best: _____

_____

_____

_____

*Sometimes silence between two friends speaks to
the heart as the whisper of an angel.*

Place photo here

Memories of a
special friend are
always heavenly.

Place photo here

When I
count my blessings
at Christmas ...

Love Peace

Joy

Place photo here

Christmas comes
but once a year—
memories stay in
our hearts forever.

Place photo here

memories...simply the best:

My angel's a little tattered...
Not as starry-eyed as she used to be...
With her patched-up wings, she's still flying...
and watching over me.

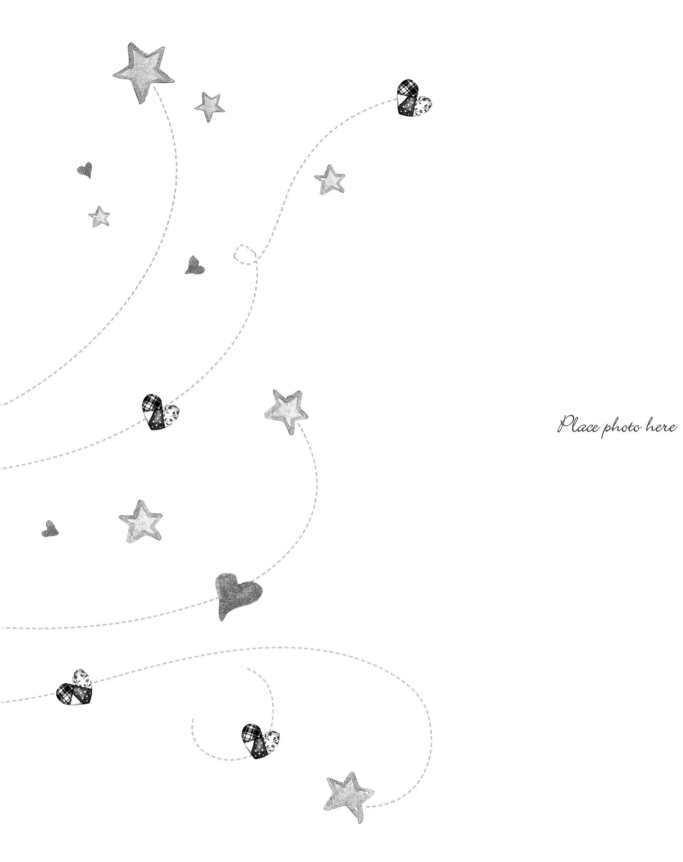

Place photo here

Just as two hearts are better
than one, memories shared
with a friend are
better than anything!

Place photo here

You gave me wings...

memories...simply the best:

Place photo here

A robin builds her nest
in happy anticipation of the
memories it will hold
after it is empty.

Place photo here

Everybody needs a little T.L.C. ....

Place photo here

Let your spirits soar with
happy memories just as if
they were being carried on
the wings of angels.

Place photo here

memories…simply the best:

10. They let you borrow stuff

9. Shopping helper!

8. Secret keepers

7. Someone to share JOY

6. Someone to share SORROW

5. They come to your plastic-ware party!

4. If you order dessert…they will, too!

3. They let you whine

2. They're always on your side

1. Giggles…giggles…giggles!

10 Reasons to love a friend…

Place photo here

Rather than merely
remembering the gift,
how much better to fill
our hearts with
memories of the giver.

Place photo here

'Tis the "wee little" deeds of kindness
that make friendships take wing.

Place photo here

Memories are the fabric of
friendship sewn together
with threads of faith,
hope, and harmony.

Place photo here

©'97 S.G.E.

memories...simply the best:

Life is a parade!
Grab a friend and hitch up your wagon!

Place photo here

Friends may come and
friemds may go, but memories
of these friendships will
stay and shine forever.

Place photo here

memories...simply the best:

Broadcast seeds of kindness on
the wind...some of them will
blossom into friends.

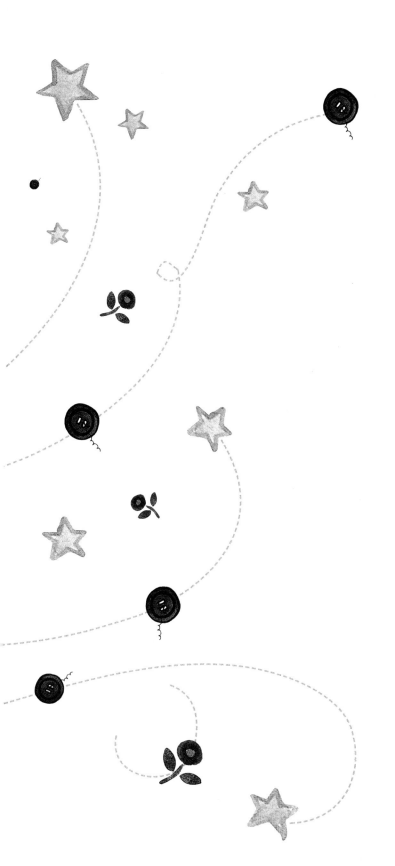

Place photo here

Plant memories deep in the soil
of your heart and they will
bloom even bigger and better.

Place photo here

Love's the buzz!

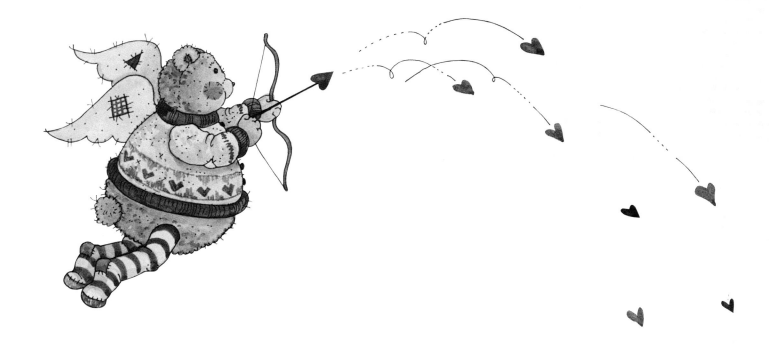

Place photo here

Even when I'm sleeping,
my dreams are
filled with happy memories.

Place photo here

memories...simply the best:

Let us dance...let us sing...
let our spirits set to wing...

Place photo here

Even on a cloudy day,
memories of special times
and special places
always shine through.

Place photo here

memories...simply the best:

Celebrating you is such a joyful thing to do!

Place photo here

Birthdays come and
birthdays go,
but memories of true
friemds stay with us always!

Place photo here

About the Artist

Sandi Gore Evans divides her busy life between her own gallery, and the magnificent watercolors that celebrate her everyday life. She grew up with a keen interest in art, encouraged by her father, a "Sunday" painter who had a great love for the arts. A self-taught artist, Sandi finds inspirations for her compositions in the things that surround her—fresh-picked strawberries and flowers, a Valentine from a friend, those ever-present angels, or yummy chocolate chip cookies just out of the oven.

She spends her days at the Gore-Evans Gallery in Augusta, Kansas, as well as enjoying her grandchildren and often working on her paintings until the wee hours of the morning. Sandi's paintings clearly reflect the joy she finds in her life, her work, her family, and her home.

May it always be raining violets...